D0746871

BACH
to the
FUTURE

Fostering Music Literacy Today

JARROD RICHEY

RET U NE
PUBLICATIONS
MONROE, LOUISIANA

Printed in the United States of America

First Printing, 2016

ISBN 978-0-692-72934-2

RETUNE PUBLICATIONS
Monroe, Louisiana

www.retunepublications.org
www.bachtothefuture.info

Sarah Macrery

wife, best friend and inspiration

CONTENTS

Preface

From the outset, this book will presuppose the fact that Jesus Christ is Lord of all, and from that flows all profitable methods of instruction and living. If that is an irreconcilable difficulty for you, this book is not for you. If you are a Christian and/or music educator like me, struggling to find helpful and concise guidelines to meet the growing need for music training in churches, schools and communities, then hold on as we go through some principles together to guide such instruction.

I will put forth some of my thoughts and suggestions as they pertain to music training and the real need for music literacy in our culture today. There are many things that could be addressed in a book like this, but I have chosen to highlight the ones most important in the discussion of music literacy. I speak as one who is in the midst of this work and not someone who is writing from the sidelines. The scope of this book is meant to be primarily practical and accessible for those who are in a similar situation. I make no pretense to have exhaustive years of understanding on music, and I stand on the shoulders of men and women who do have greater understanding of this subject and its ramifications than I do. I speak with a voice that is asking some of the same questions that others have asked and continue to ask in recent years. These questions can be summarized in this one question, "how shall we train our children in music?"

I write this in an effort to bring thoughtful, joyful music literacy training to the forefront of the conversation. It has been relegated to the periphery, sometimes unintentionally. My hope is that this work will spark even more conversation among parents and educators alike. I hope that from this book comes a desire to read the faithful writings of men and women who have not only written about music education but who have rolled their sleeves up and done the business of training musicians, many without even being noticed. I write to you now as one who has both sleeves rolled up and is facing the day-to-day challenges of not just training *about* music but more fervently training people to *do* music. For this reason I offer this handbook of sorts, as a call and encouragement for continued and renewed subjection of all understanding of music training, education and practice under the will of the Triune God.

JARROD RICHEY

Trinity Season, 2016

INTRODUCTION:
Bach or Bust

To be forthright, this is not a book about Bach. It is one, however, seeking to recognize the influences and circumstances of such a great composer to prepare and produce greater Bachs to arise and advance the mission of the Church as he did. Bach was a culture maker, a creator. He drastically changed the trajectory of western music culture by setting a higher standard. A glance around current music culture will find few men able to compose music with such great Scriptural understanding and skill. Why is that the case? Where are the stalwart stewards of Christ-centered music today? The purpose of this book is to foster a return to music literacy, using the example of Bach as a lens that can provide some clarity and perspective to future generations seeking to serve their Creator in greater musical endeavors. Introducing him will shed light on some of the things lost in modern music training.

The first thing to highlight is the fact that Johann Sebastian Bach was a baptized Christian, born one hundred and sixty-eight years after Martin Luther's famous 95 Theses were tacked onto the door at the Wittenberg Cathedral. This is significant because the reformation of worship and theology of the Church had been ongoing, in and around what is now Germany and surrounding regions for over a century and a half by the time that Sebastian Bach would begin his study as a musician. Bach was born into a time that was Christian in name and practice. Lutheranism was the official religion throughout the region. This is what Bach knew. This is where he was reared. Bach was born a Christian, lived, worked and died a Christian. This is how he must be perceived to understand the lasting power of his work.

Modern Christians are surrounded by people who prefer that faith be confined to the space between the ears, far away from any actual practice or life habits. There are those who downplay the strength of Bach's faith and devotion. This kind of revision is often self-serving or overreaching. He is reduced to an austere bust separated from his faithful life of service to the Church. In truth, his Christianity was crucial to his creational success.

Despite what current caretakers of Bach's musical catalogue might tell you, Bach was not an academic by modern standards. He was not a university professor or composer-in-residence at the Thuringian (or central German) equivalent of the leading secular university's music school. Today, certain historians and musicologists would have you imagine Bach working in the same career path as they, or worse, operating aristocratically above others of his time, not truly embracing the political and social practice of his day. When the majority of people trained in music are taught at a public university, this misunderstanding becomes entrenched. The current bust of Sebastian Bach has become an idol which serves the ideals and agenda of modern musicians who mold him into a mirror of themselves. But Bach did not live and learn in a day and age like our own. He did not receive his foundational music instruction in a secular university, with the Church relegated to the background of arts and culture as it is today. He did not perform the majority of his compositions in the secular concert hall. The majority of his work was composed for use in the worship of the Church.

It is both because Bach was steeped in the theology of his faith and was highly skilled at his craft that he put out such incredible works. The natural marriage of these two things is all but forgotten. This book is meant to show the need to revive a full-bodied training in music today, one that imparts great skill while simultaneously instructing the student musicians in that which will elevate their creating of music in greater imitation of the Great Composer. Music must be taught again in the context of God's Word. If current music instruction aligns itself with the training practices of Bach's day, the Triune God will raise up greater Bachs in the coming generations to sound his glory anew. It is a model for how we might bring *Bach to the future.*

THE GOAL OF
MUSIC LITERACY

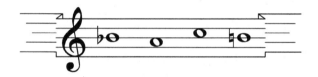

Moderns, as children of the microwave generation, prefer the quickest solution, the just add water, stir and heat variety being particularly praised. When it comes to music, there is a similar expectation for a guaranteed recipe, one to evenly divide over school lesson plans and watch as literate musicians magically appear over time. The error in this approach lies in the fact that a truly literate musician is never a quick product, nor is it easy. Schools train vastly different crops of students, located in culturally different parts of the country with various family and church backgrounds. There are never going to be identical students at the same level and ability able to learn at the exact same pace and formula. It is important to resist the temptation to codify and be too narrow in how music literacy is accomplished. And, truth be told, identical musicians that roll off the factory lines of schools should not even be the goal.

The goal is to have musicians trained in the most faithful and efficient manner to accomplish the most with the gifts the Lord has given them. Whether or not each one turns out to be a career musician is only an incidental detail. The goal is not training musicians so that they can be music majors in college and get a good job. It is training them to be who they are—image bearers of the Triune God. In order to be full imitators of God, students need to learn how to be musicians themselves, able to read, write and create music. They will live all their days as worshipers and image bearers of their Heavenly Father.

As evidenced today, the education system that does not center itself around the Gospel of Jesus Christ will find no lasting attraction to music and art. Satan knows the strong power of music and the threat it poses to Kingdom dominion. That is why determination must be ever-vigilant in thinking about music and its ability to reflect not only God, but also what god(s) society is serving. As students venture out into the world, regardless of what vocational calling they pursue, they must be musicians if only for one day a week, the Lord's Day, to show the world who God is. Therefore, music literacy will serve them simply because they are Christian.

Once a culture starts to restore the priority of training children in music, the task shifts to finding what type of instruction should be present in formal school education. It is a modern mindset to over-compartmentalize disciplines in education. When it comes to music, the resulting tendency is to see it as a stand alone subject. While it can be a subject all by itself, it would be better to liken music to a language. When a language is taught, there is focus on the grammar, literature, creative writing and so forth. Language is strengthened in more places than just English class. Since music literacy in the fullest sense is the end goal, programs need to be purposefully structured to accomplish this. School leadership must be constantly evaluating how their students are being trained in music. Are the students being mere receptacles of music? Or are they doers and re-creators of music? If the latter, then music instruction will be diverse, multifaceted and braided into the culture of the school. A few concerts and a bit of knowledge about music notes will not equip students for lifelong music creating after their Creator.

Since there is no simple formula to churn out musically literate students, does that suggest that strict standards and overarching principles cannot be found? Absolutely not. In fact, there should be principles that guide music instruction as well as an understanding that vastly different methods and practices can still operate well under those principles. This is not a rejection of fixed standards. Instead, it is a call to unify around shared principles (rather than method preferences) all the while aiming together at the goal of raising music makers.

EVERYONE
CAN SING

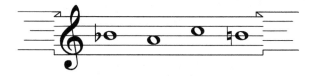

The first principle of teaching music literacy is any student can be taught to sing. Because all types of challenges can be found in a variety of students, this must be the baseline thinking of the instructor if any real progress is to be made. There will be students who have had very little exposure to music and students who have professional musicians for parents. There will be that one student that you think cannot possibly move beyond his monotoned crowing. Trust me, he can.

The tendency is to think that the ability to do music is something a person is either born with or not. People are born with the ability to make music and sing, provided the ears and voices are in good working order. Can everyone be Pavarotti? No, but giving up on a student too quickly will not produce results, and it will discourage them from even trying. The music teacher who has been in the game long enough will have seen that moment in a student's eyes, the moment they finally match pitch or the moment they get that difficult rhythm right after repeated failures. The goal is to try to move that student up one notch, and then another, and another. Not all of them will end up top notch, and that is fine. When ad jingles and pop radio are the extent of a family's exposure to music, it is no wonder a student seems hopeless. Maybe they heard at home "no one in this family can carry a tune." Far too many people have bought into the idea that basic singing ability is selectively distributed among the population. The teacher has to be the one to think differently and to give such a student new shoulders to stand on along with a few more steps to climb on the music literacy ladder. Saying everyone can sing is not the same thing as saying everyone can sing easily. It will be hard work.

MUSIC AS LANGUAGE

Comparing learning music to language instruction is helpful. All people are born with the ability to learn Chinese or German. But if a person is born in the United States, ordinarily, they would not be exposed to the Chinese or German language enough in those first months to become fluent. Music works the same way. Children need to be saturated with singing and music making from their earliest years at home. Even if they are not, then the school programs can still provide a potent mixture of music saturation to help fortify their musicianship. But make no mistake, they all possess the ability to make music and sing at some level. Saying that a student does not have a musical gene is like saying a child does not have the gene for learning Spanish. A student who enters your school at age 9 ½ will have a steeper climb than those who have had exposure to good music. Just as it would be harder for a 35-year old to begin to study Chinese or German for the first time, so it is difficult to begin studying music for the first time once past those early years for saturation. If instruction coalesces around the principle that everyone can sing and make music, then teaching can be tailored to maximize the potential of each set of students. Then, if taught as a language, music immersion will steadily push them toward its use. Quantity of time with the students will support this language comparison. Twice a week for 30 minutes is not much of a language immersion experience. As much time as possible should be given for music instruction.

WHEN A TOUGH CASE COMES ALONG

It is encouraging to remember that literacy has multiple aspects. When there is a particularly challenging crop of young musicians, be assured that, though it may take more work and a slower pace, there is no reason to give up the instruction. Applying the principle that "everyone can sing" will change from year to year and school to school. There are always new students who further complicate the issue. Even an established student with good understanding of intervals between notes, could lag in participation because he can not match pitch with his own voice. Still others may sing well, but not grasp the solfege between the sung notes.

A new 4th grader who cannot match pitch may drop into your school's established music class. Ideally, the teacher will want to speak with the student apart from the class and reassure him that the class will be an adjustment for him. He should participate the best he can, working and listening attentively even though he feels behind. Gradually, as the teacher leads the class, greater voice control will come through exploration and song games. Plus, the new student will be exposed to solfege and singing repetition from his peers which will only help him in his saturation deficit. These are all little pieces of what it takes to reach music literacy. The most important thing is for the teacher to be patient and reassuring to the student. Though a long process, a student who is behind can catch on and follow the way into tuneful singing.

Again, just like language study, there are different components to literacy. Comprehension of the French language will often come before the ability to speak it. The student who seems like an impossible case is often gathering some of the components of music literacy long before the fruits are evident. The teacher and the student must understand that music comprehension and production will not always grow equally. The teacher should be encouraged that with continued saturation, the struggling student will likely be gathering the material well before he may be able to sing tunefully in class activities.

THREE-LEGGED STOOL:
Progression of Hearing, Doing, Understanding

The second principle to guide the administration of music curriculum and instruction is that music instruction best follows the progression of hearing and doing, then understanding. This starts immediately as students' ears are filled with songs in their schooling, the "hearing" step. Teachers who can model correct pitch and technique will be giving a good introduction to music for their young singers. Following a good model in their teacher, students are then invited to participate as they explore their own voices. This is the "doing" stage. The third stage of "understanding" comes after students have begun to make music with their own voices. It is embedded in them, making them ready to understand the concepts a particular song demonstrates. This is the natural pattern in all language learning.

HEARING AND DOING

The first two stages, "hearing" and "doing," focus on saturation, pouring in as much good music material as possible. In the earliest years, this includes song stories, nursery rhymes, song games, movement activities and more. Have the youngest singers learn simple folk songs like "Ring Around the Rosie," "A Tisket, A Tasket," "Rain, Rain, Go Away," and other similar songs that help them sing and grow into their voice. Often these same songs provide movement or game opportunities to help them in their motor skill development as well. Ideally, this starts with a young class of kindergarten or first graders. They can learn 50-75 simple folk songs and rhymes in their formal music class times. The movements too must be age appropriate for them. Students love very simple circle movement and chase activities helping them learn and play at the same time.

This same pattern holds regardless of the beginning age of the student. Naturally, the speed, motor skills and cognitive abilities differ from a first to an eighth grader, so the pattern must hold in more creative and subtle ways. When a middle school teacher is handed a class of 7th graders who have never had any formal music literacy curriculum, "Ring Around the Rosie" or even "Hot Cross Buns" will neither challenge nor excite them. Plus, they likely will not have even heard of some of these simple folk songs and rhymes. Instead, this fresh crop of older singers could start by reading from simple intervals and solfege singing exercises pulled from folk songs in any number of singing exercise books. These same songs can be introduced as a mystery song with simple rhythm and melody on a staff. The teacher can give the students the starting solfege sound and set the beat for them. The challenge of trying to sing or identify new songs can be motivating to these young singers. It is also invigorating to the teacher to see them starting to read music, especially if they could not do it at all when they entered the program. Teaching them to read songs on solfege using Curwen hand signs or body signs can be the quickest way to get them engaged in reading music. Motions, movements, games and other activities disguise the learning and distract them from thinking it is a childish chore.

The "hearing" and "doing" parts of the process can also be reinforced throughout the school day, outside the formal music classroom. Any profitable music being played immerses the students deeper into the language of music. Whether you are a music teacher or an administrator, as you have opportunity, encourage a musical culture beyond classroom time. Does your school use chant and song for memory work? Shirley Method jingles for grammar? Is convocation/chapel time basically announcements and prayer? Why not sing the Doxology or a verse of the school hymn or anthem? Encourage more singing as a student body. Keep up with events in your area: musicals, symphony concerts, operas. Hand out this information to give students more opportunities to hear music. For those with little or no music background, these bursts of music immersion will help them learn its language and make the teacher's job a little easier.

UNDERSTANDING

Once music is embedded into the students, they will be ready for "understanding." Even the youngest students can be taught to recognize the difference between high/ low, fast/slow, loud/soft and similar concepts that set the stage for understanding more complex examples of same/different distinctions in future materials. This basic discernment comes from being able to sing, tap, feel, move and find the differences in the music. In the earliest music classes these young students are invited to tap on their legs or on any number of new instruments to learn to feel the heartbeat of the music being sung by the teacher. The student needs to experience the feel of the heartbeat for themselves as opposed to only hearing or seeing the teacher demonstrate this. The approach is continued like building blocks. For instance, the teacher using both hearing and feeling, prepares students to make conscious the solfege syllable "fa." As they sing the mystery sound until it is named, and as that day draws closer the mystery sound's body sign location is repeatedly demonstrated to go along with what they had been hearing. It is through these varied methods of movement that specific musical concepts are introduced, identified and made naturally conscious over time—all while providing the teacher visual assessment of which students are understanding and which students may be struggling to grasp the concept. The oldest students will have enough material established from previous training to receive a simple, verbal explanation for some of the concepts.

Introducing musical abstractions without grounding the students in song material leaves them with disconnected terms; like telling a first grader that "sol" down to "mi" is a minor third interval before actually letting him experience it. There is no context or category for him to understand that. Instead, well-learned songs in the mind of a student provide a wealth of lesson material because the student is able to hear, feel and experience the concept being taught. A song like "Hot Cross Buns" can be great for teaching the quarter rest concept in the first grade and then can be revisited to teach the solfege syllable "re" in the second grade. The progression is a natural one if songs are used in a gradually accelerating sequence. This progression continues throughout the timeline of a student's education. If brought through this type of training from the start, the older students will be ready for understanding harder concepts of music theory and composition as well as be reading music. They will at last be reaping the hard earned fruits of music literacy.

HOW THE ONE-LEGGED STOOL FALLS

Following the progression of hearing, doing, then understanding, will not only ensure a more musically literate generation, it will also guard against some of the pitfalls currently present in music classes across the country. If these sound anything like what is happening at your school, perhaps it is time to revisit the music program goals.

Performance Pressures

The first pitfall is giving in to performance pressure at the expense of true music training. In other words, it is the "doing" of music without the "hearing" and "understanding." Today's musically illiterate generation wants to see the fruits of literacy without patience for the process. Everybody wants to see their baby in the limelight. Maybe the school board wants evidence that the new music program is working. What better proof than to trot the students out on the stage and have a concert? Plus, there is the additional temptation of the Facebook video. Mom and Dad want a special moment to post for Grandma.

The trouble with this pitfall is subtle because concerts and performances are not bad things in and of themselves. In fact, they are very good things. Too often, the music teacher feels pressure to have a choir perform in order to justify their work. The teacher will likely have to line out the parts and rely on rote teaching to get to a performance. But without having the students read and work through the piece to a degree themselves, their music literacy and musical independence will not be strengthened. If literacy is truly the goal then the students must be constantly working towards reading for themselves in the choral rehearsal.

Addressing this issue requires a shift in focus on the part of more than just the music teacher, but small changes from the teacher can start the process. If performances are inevitable, pick some rounds or canons and have them accompanied with available instruments rather than grabbing a SAB or SATB choir octavo and teaching each part by rote from the piano bench. The round or canon can be heard, read and analyzed in a short amount of time and will provide building blocks for growth of the young singers. Or, in a way similar to having the student echo back the sentence in their first grade reader, have the choir simply echo back the phrase or passage being played on the piano. If handed an inexperienced group of junior high or high school singers, think "less is more."

There is more opportunity for success in music literacy if material is chosen that sets the class up for growth. Overwhelming them with expectations to perform a grand choir anthem merely because of their age cripples them for future growth after the big concert. They will not be able to read, write or understand the complex concepts in music they are singing and may very well depart your school musically illiterate. Keeping the concert repertoire simple will allow more class time to introduce basic literacy concepts. Introducing more literacy tools will then make future concerts easier to prepare.

Another way to alleviate performance pressure is by giving an onstage demonstration of what the students are already doing in class rather than preparing a separate performance piece. An event where other classes are showing memory work, speeches, math drills, etc… take a few slots to demonstrate a solfege drill, dance or rhythm game. This gives parents a brief glimpse into the music training without taking away from valuable class time to prepare something extra.

Music History vs. Music Making

A second pitfall in music classes today is teaching music history instead of teaching the skills for making music. Music classes of recent decades replace music training with fine arts surveys on the lives and music of the great composers. Sounds great, right? And at first, this appears to be quite academic. But this approach does not give students the ability to make the music that the great composers would have been able to make. If music classes have students listening to music by Bach, reading about his birthplace and genealogy, but do not leave them with the ability to read and sing some portion of the music Bach wrote, then the approach is out of balance. This is a common tendency, and at best, it is only the "hearing" leg of the stool.

In addition, this also squanders the most crucial years of musical development for the student. If music is reduced to a history class, then there is no rush to teach it to young children. They can always learn about the composers in college. The result of this is a bunch of musically illiterate college freshmen taking music appreciation classes, a far less likely crowd to be moved to greater music making and learning at the age of eighteen than back when they were a classroom full of eager eight year olds.

Returning to the language metaphor, a 35 year old hearing about the Chinese language can only gain so much appreciation from having it described to him. If he is not given the ability to experience and speak it, then it will quickly lose its luster. In music making and beginning singing, the student will obtain the ability to develop what they have learned. Why overly explain music when students can grow to love it through experience? If they cannot start at a young age, then fast track them through some singing and music making sequences mixing that in with history and context as needed. The three-legged stool of music literacy must be the principle against which curricular methods are tested. Students need to hear and do, then understand. Knowing *about* music is not enough. The main component in training students should be training them to make music themselves.

Now, lest anyone think music appreciation classes are the bad guy, think of them as a bridge for a generation of students who have not been exposed to great music at home or in their culture. It is not a waste, but must be seen as one small part of the equation for music literacy. The 21st century high school and college student can name several of the top songs by pop artists but cannot name or hum the tune of two of the top songs by J.S. Bach, Beethoven or Mozart.

Applied understanding of the principles of music literacy means making sure that a music appreciation class does not take the place of training in how to think and sing music. The biography and historical context of the great composers can be gleaned from reading books in other subjects, but a balanced curriculum that understands the place of music will make sure students are constantly being instructed in *doing* music in addition to learning *about* music.

MUSICAL CHAIRS

Understanding that every school is at a different level musically and has different resources, how can a suitable method be chosen? As long as the principles of the three legged stool remain, there is room for variety. No checklist can be uniformly applied. Instead, constant assessment and adjustment are required to see if a method fits a particular group.

One particular approach closely follows the pattern of hearing, doing, then understanding using the stages of Prepare, Present and Practice. These are the stages of the Kodály (pronounced "CODE-eye") methodology of music instruction. "Prepare" takes the form of singing and teaching students a piece of folk music. Here, concepts are modeled for the child before he has words to describe them. "Present" is the quickest stage in that it is the naming and contextualizing of what the student has been doing in songs and games up to that point. The hearing and doing are masked in fun and play and become the equivalent to emersion in a language. From here, the "Practice" phase takes over as the student explores the same song material in varied ways like reading the song in music notation, writing the song down, and identifying the song material in other types of songs. All of this culminates in students gaining understanding of the concepts within the music.

Hungarian composer and musicologist, Zoltán Kodály, understood that the music and culture of the people must be harnessed to train them, an approach that is easily inserted into American instruction. Where Kodály would start with a certain set of folk songs from Hungary, American folk songs can be used to transfer the concepts more fully here. Kodály's philosophy (that the music of the people is the best and most accessible material for training students) allows flexibility in the order of what specific concepts and folk songs are used. The goal remains to train musicians to be fully literate. Other methods will have differing ways to accomplish this, but the Kodály methodology and approach to training young musicians remains one of the strongest options.

There are other methods that offer music literacy tools for teachers. The Swiss composer and music educator Émile Jaques-Dalcroze's method of music training is often referred to as eurythmics. Dalcroze's movement emphasis is helpful to the teacher who is trying to train students to think, feel, and sing the different types of rhythms and harmonies in music. Another method, the Orff-Schulwerk Method from German composer Carl Orff, provides kinesthetic opportunities for musicianship. The student can learn by doing in an atmosphere of play. This is accomplished with percussion instruments commonly referred to as Orff instruments. Both of these methods seek after greater music literacy and skill and can be used in complementary ways with some of the Kodály methodology. The skillful teacher armed with proper focus on literacy can use as many of tools from these methods and philosophies as possible. No single method is infallible. All require wisdom in application.

YOU ARE WHAT
YOU SING

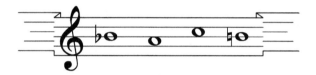

Music is not just for the ears. It is for the whole body, which involves the soul. Just as the phrase, "you are what you eat" is more than the basic science of mealtime, so the third principle in music instruction is more than notes and soundwaves. You are what you sing. Like a good diet, the best musical material lends itself to the healthiest learning for the student. That means it must be varied, accessible and helpful in training. Using only high-art, concert music is not well balanced just as a diet of only fine steak leaves out many nutrients. The musical diet of the student must be considered in this way if healthy music literacy is going to be achieved.

WORD-CENTERED MUSICIANS

As Christian students are learning what it means to be people of the Word, they must experience music that reflects the Word of God as it is—rich, layered, textured and purposeful. If students are exposed to music of this merit, they will learn lessons beyond the notes they sing. A varied musical diet enables students to better understand the Triune God. The words that dwell in the Christian are important since out of the heart the mouth speaks. Good music training will lend itself to spiritual maturity given its connections to the Scriptures and its ability to carry multiple meanings simultaneously. As what students take in and put out musically will shape them, so being singers of the Word will shape them for good. Music is one of the most useful tools to help Christians understand the Bible. Keeping that perspective in the classroom certainly inspires wise selection of lesson content.

This balance can be upset when Christians wrongly seek to "christianize" all reading and singing material. Being singers of the Word does not mean only singing words from the Bible. The temptation in this area is to be reactionary to what is happening in surrounding culture. In an effort to shield students from the bad stuff out there, a teacher today might choose only Christian music and jingles for music training in the Christian school—a limited diet indeed! While the intention sounds right, Christians of the last four decades have sacrificed musical maturity as a result. When lyrics are overvalued and music structure devalued, then music maturity cannot flourish. If the music is seen merely as a vessel to carry words, then why have anything but the most basic tunes and forms? Why would there be a need to marry form to content? Of course, a reverse trend of only the latest hip music will fail just the same. Balance is essential.

When a full understanding of the Word is lacking, Christians tend to judge songs as either holy or unholy, sacred or secular. The Dutch theologian, Abraham Kuyper, is famous in many Christian circles for saying, "There is not a square inch in the whole domain of our human existence over which Christ, who is Sovereign over all, does not cry, 'Mine!'" That means that Jesus is Lord over all music as well. Musical practice and maturity involves working with a growing understanding of that fact. Maturity must not be neglected in the name of a falsely pious spirituality. Instead, correct the modern tendency among Christian educators to use mediocre song material simply because the lyrics are religious. This is a poor diet.

Again, applying the language analogy to music instruction, students do not need to be reading only Bible stories and Psalms when language is being taught. Sacred and secular texts alike are profitable for study. In a sense, all reading practice and strengthening of language skills is geared towards literacy of The Word incarnate and His Scriptures. So music training is geared toward worshipping and reflecting the Word incarnate.

STORY SINGERS

Beyond being people of the Word, students need to understand how to use good words in the way God uses them. He is the first and greatest storyteller. As God sings over His creation and tells its story, the music is inaudible to His creatures as they move about, yet He is clearly communicating His faithfulness in word and deed. Over the smallest crawling crustacean or largest cloud-wrapped mountain, He sings. Music should be reflective of the great and glorious God of the universe—Someone worth imitating indeed. When God composes, it is a massive symphony of sound and texture. He uses the entire sonic landscape in His creational composition, taking His time, varying and developing the themes. In one story, a child loses his mother, darkness and quiet prevail in the theme. Volume and triumph might dominate the story of a wayward son embracing repentance and becoming energized to share the Good News with others. In Scripture, God's people have long demonstrated this diversity. King David cries out in desperation in Psalm 22 because he cannot hear God. Yet the Great Storyteller turns his mourning into dancing and cries of joy in Psalm 30. Singing as God sings must include this great variety and interwoven nature of storytelling.

Well paired beauty and harmony and lyrics demonstrate the nature of the greatest composer, the Heavenly Creator. So in the smaller scale of the classroom, the solfege patterns of "Rain, Rain Go Away" introduce a child to the mathematical order God placed in music. Or the high school student is awed by the magic of fivefold harmony from his classmates as they work through a piece of music. It does not have to be a high performance art to be good for the student's soul or to teach him about his God, but it needs to be a steady progression over his education from playful folk song to grand symphony. By the end of his formal education a student should understand the Word in many and diverse ways. But he must be shown God's glory in song, both in lyrics and in the music that carries it along.

What does this mean practically in the classroom? Students need a rich musical diet. They need to consume good word and story. Chants, hymns, folk songs, grand choruses, all of it feeds them. As they mature musically, they need to experience singing polyphony from composers like Bach, Handel and Vivaldi, so that they can see how such composers image God, writing many voices chasing one another in imitative and contrasting ways. The Master Composer takes many lives and voices and weaves them into a Gospel harmony, a greater good, both at the personal and cosmic levels. If students are taught music with this in mind, they mature in their understanding of their Creator.

A BREATHING
CURRICULUM

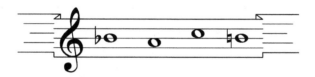

The next principle for imparting full music literacy is to recognize the teacher as a living, breathing curriculum. The person teaching the students will be a standard for them no matter what method or textbook is being used. As in other fields of study, music students will seek to emulate what is presented before them.

In the days of J.S. Bach, students wanted to be apprenticed to master musicians so that they might glean all they could from them. A textbook was not the normal mode for music training. Rather, the teacher's work, actions and words comprised the curriculum. Bach famously walked over 250 miles in the fall of 1705, from

Arnstadt to Lubeck in approximately ten days to hear and learn from the famous organist and composer Dietrich Buxtehude. This dedicated form of mentorship and apprenticeship needs to be embraced again today. Music has long been considered a craft to be taught by careful example and observation. Children learn to speak from the language around them. Therefore, music pupils model singing and habits of their teacher, good or bad.

ABOUT THE TEACHER

As the breathing curriculum, the first step for the teacher is to be someone worthy of emulation. This sobering reminder should motivate instructors to be more skilled musicians able to humbly and joyfully shepherd the young musicians entrusted to their care. Perfect mastery is not required, but the teacher must have more skill and knowledge than the students in order to lead them in the next step toward music maturity.

Inspires Imitation

First, not only must the teacher be worth imitating but also one who inspires imitation. In other words, a music teacher needs to have an infectious love for the discipline of music-making. A teacher who truly believes that music has deep value and centrality for a Christian's quest to imitate God will see his job as more than a paycheck. He will value the opportunity to guide the students in the world of music, excited to introduce new people to such a highly fruitful, lifelong skill. This excitement will spill out into the classroom, and stir the students to follow his example.

Is a Good Model

Second, the teacher must be able to model good singing and musicianship for the students. Tone and volume are quickly absorbed by little ears. They will be learning from their teacher's habits and level of singing ability. That does not mean that an elementary music teacher needs to be able to teach form and analysis at the college level. At the same time not just any parent volunteer or private piano teacher will be qualified to teach music literacy. Sometimes there is no other option, but schools should have a long view and choose a well-trained instructor.

In addition to good musicianship, a music teacher seeking to model well must prepare for class time thouroughly so as to sing with confidence and must understand the concepts and need for purposeful, progressive lesson planning. Music concepts must be demonstrated in an order that flows naturally upward into growth. A teacher who has worked through what it takes to become a good model in musicianship, will recognize the frame of the student before them and what they are ready to learn next.

Thinks Apprenticeship

The teacher as a breathing curriculum, must have some awareness of the model of apprenticeship. It is fostering growth in a specific set of students in a certain school in a certain time. It has to be more intentional than a stamp out button pushers mode. Not all the students will learn the same but can follow the instructor in an individual way, gleaning according to their own capabilities as the training moves along. They will want to be like their instructor. They will want to play like their instructor. This is more effective than working in a textbook for a desired result. They will naturally treat their teacher as their mentor.

Modern education puts a high premium on curricula and often misses the fact that education is about training and apprenticeship. The majority of the training of musicians in western culture happened in a time when there was no industrial printing of copies of music, books and scores. Instead, musicians would have to copy their own scores and study with master teachers and performers whom they could learn to emulate. This mode of learning produced better trained musicians.

Music teachers in schools today should use resources and curriculum books to help and guide them along the way, but should remember that music training is not about making carbon copy musicians. It is about training and shaping individual children made in the image of God. The more teachers realize and work as if they are mentoring their students, the more transformative their music classrooms will be.

NOW WHAT?

If you are an administrator, how do you find teachers to operate this way in your school? Many qualities of such a teacher can be checked when hiring for a position. Look for someone joyful and hardworking who can sing tunefully and skillfully. Can they do it without accompaniment so as to teach games, etc? Do not assume that music literacy can be attained by simply hiring a skilled pianist or instrumentalist or choir director. Have a music teacher candidate lead a short lesson with a group of students. Watch them interact and hear how they sing and sound. Once hired, the music teacher's best reinforcement is support from the school leadership. Check in on progress and see that the vision is being pursued. Point donors and sponsors to the program so the classroom can be filled with instruments and tools for multi-faceted music literacy. Help saturate the school's culture with music by advocating more singing as a student body and in the individual classrooms. Talk about the importance of music training to parents, grandparents and school supporters. Do not leave all the music advocacy to the music teacher.

If you are a music teacher, how do you restart now? Begin by solidifying a vision for music literacy. Check that your strategy upholds the three legged stool of how students best learn music: hearing, doing, understanding. Surround yourself with colleagues who are in similar work so that there can be encouragement and help in the tough business of trying to train young students to be fully literate. Email groups, Facebook groups, conferences and

$\equiv$ 45 $\equiv$

regional workshops can provide a source of inspiration and community that will prove essential in this endeavor. From these sources one can find the necessary material for implementing new literacy ideas. Then make it a priority to give students rich content and be excited about it to them. Continue to be a student of music yourself, so that you always have a bit more to offer as mentor.

It is transformational to give students the tools to recreate music and not just observe it. Imagine their ability to understand the world and the Triune God in light of a musical understanding. Think of what an understanding of music structure can bring your students when they are not only able to hear prolonged tension and delayed resolution in cantatas and symphonies but also hear it in light of the grand story in which they live. Imagine how with such an understanding, they can re-echo the gospel in new ways like the great composers and hymn writers of the church have done in times past. Think of the new settings of Psalm tunes that can be written. Think about several generations being able to learn music from an early age in a way similar to how they learn the English language. Think of a time when most people have music training growing up, and "I'm just not gifted in music" is no longer a common sentiment. Think of a baseline of music education in our Christian culture that allows us to be more like our musical Creator in His music-filled world.

Imagine the singing abilities of our congregations on the Lord's Day if the majority in attendance can read any music put before them. Imagine the multitude of ways the glories of God's goodness can be echoed and resounded through settings of psalms, hymns, and spiritual songs by the coming generations. Imagine moving from glory to glory in compositions like Haydn's *Creation* or Bach's *St. Matthew Passion* to greater compositions that stand on the shoulders of these great composers. Work so that your students will understand the glorious skill in such works and can see the attributes of God in its excellence. Work so that they are given the gift of music literacy, able to read and participate in similar pieces of music themselves. Imagine your students' great-grandchildren growing and maturing in their faith and understanding of God's creation in light of the faithful stewardship of music around them.

If you are patient, the future fruits of your teaching will lend great strength to the kingdom as you release students with musical abilities to worship and to create music with skill. More than bringing *Bach to the future*, it will be transforming musical maturity for greater Bachs to reflect God's unending glory from age to age.

APPENDIX A:
The Helpful Musician

Ideally, the teacher is also a musician, of course, but this more specifically addresses the musician who may or may not call himself a teacher. In fact, the musician is always a teacher, for he is always modeling something. The musician stands as a mentor to the culture around him. Music maturity in a culture requires two things from musicians.

First, it requires that musicians step out of *academia* and be willing to speak of music to those who are not trained in the language of music. Many skilled musicians are unwilling to give up the secret handshakes and code words of the inner circle because it feels nice to know something that many do not know. Elitism and snobbery are common temptations for career musicians.

The fundamental problem with this attitude is that it is rooted in the idea that music and art are for the few and not for the masses. Zoltán Kodály and others like him believed and repeated the mantra of "music for all." Music is not just for the musician; it is for all people. Music by its very nature is a public, outward art. It is meant to be communal, and the attempts to keep its meaning and value accessible to a select few should be consciously avoided, especially if there is going to be any real traction in reviving a culture of people who are musically literate. The visual arts world demonstrates the current disconnect well. Imagine a twelve by twelve foot white canvas with only two grey dots slightly left of center. Is such a painting for the people or for the artist community? More often today, it is for the latter. The painters gather around the exhibit praising one another for the clarity with which this piece images the inner struggle between one's true self and what others see. The casual couple carry their glasses of merlot and steps up to the painting seeing only two grey dots. How does the artist community respond? Commonly, they respond with disdain for the couple's lack of taste and insight. Whether it is in physical or temporal art a divisive attitude of the 'haves' toward the 'have nots' is unhelpful. Musicians, like artists, need to be able to speak and create in a way that attracts other people to come into the circle.

Second, music maturity in a culture requires that the skilled help the unskilled. When musicians try to recruit people only from their insulated cliques of academia, the divide is widened further between those who can make music and those who cannot. Musicians must go out and seek to put music where the people are and try to bring them along to greater understanding. As the Scriptures remind us, to whom "much is given, much is required." The burden is on those who are musical to help those who are not. Though not an automatic fix, musicians need to be the first to move and take responsibility for music maturity if progress is going to be made. If a culture's skilled musicians are lamenting the decline of their influence in the broader modern culture, but lamenting within the confines of their own community insulated from the masses, the people will not be inspired to follow.

To follow these requirements for music maturity in a culture, the musician has a particular temptation to overcome. In the music world, accolades are currency. Attaining recognition becomes the measure of success. The Biblical pattern is always to move from glory to glory, a pattern that teaches death to self and service to others so that others might follow in greater, more glorious ways. Taking up such a pattern in music training requires humility, patience, sacrifice and service, not the most glamorous of traits in the mind of the modern musician.

As previously mentioned, the musician's job must be to imitate God, the Master Composer, performing in a way that calls for an even more glorious development of the melody by those who follow him. Modern musicians would do well to look to the lives of the great composers like Bach, Handel, Haydn and others before the Romantic period, who saw themselves as servants to God and king. Bach worked in his day without a fan club. His life and death were simple and inglorious. It was later when composers had the perspective of time that the work and service of Bach was seen for what it richly contributed. This should encourage faithfulness with a long view in serving through the calling of music making. Striving towards a similar narrative of faithfulness could be the catalyst that brings *Bach to the future.*

APPENDIX B:
To the Parents

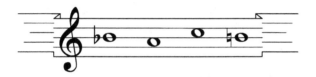

I f raising a generation of music makers is the goal, then the parents have primary responsibility in this endeavor as chief stewards of their offspring to show them the glory of God and teach them to enjoy Him forever. Their Creator God is musical. He sings over His creation. Full and complete education in the nurture and admonition of the Lord includes saturation in music, the artful language of the Father.

Many Christians have an awareness of this concept, but do not fully understand what it means to transmit a love of music to their children and effectively equip them to be musicians themselves. Regardless of their own abilities, parents have many tools at their disposal to aid in the task. If a parent wants their child to be able to sing and progress in music, there are a few important things to keep in mind when it comes to training children to re-echo the Gospel through singing.

A FATHER WHO SINGS

It might come as a wake-up call to some that music education does not begin in school. It begins in the home. Christian parents, especially Christian fathers, need to remember that they are a little picture of their Heavenly Father to their children. Singing is not something that is delegated to a select few. It is central to the Christian's identity. As such, it should be a part of the Christian home from the start.

I address the men here because often they are the ones shying away from music. The leaders are leading poorly. If we are going to continue to mature in our callings as faithful husbands and fathers, we must reject the idea that men do not sing. We have become confused on what is masculine and feminine in our current cultural climate, so why would we take our cue from that? Modern stereotypes paint singing as an image of weakness, lacking glory and strength. In reality, singing and making music are just the opposite. It requires strength and glory and discipline and training to be done well. It is a tool of warfare in the kingdom. One of the greatest warriors in the Bible was also one of its greatest musicians, King David. The Triune God Himself is the Alpha Singer. If it is good enough for the Father, it must be good enough for lesser fathers here on earth. We would do well to consider singing as human—both masculine and feminine. So, rightly understood, singing is a normal activity for men who are made in the image of God. If a dad is holding back in this area, so will the offspring in his house. As Christian men repent of this apathy, they will reorient their music practice in submission to the Father's example. They will give themselves to music maturity and singing. They will feed a desire to learn more about God's musical order and seek to experience more of it. They will raise sons and daughters who are able to sing skillfully and joyfully. Their homes will be full of holy recreation which imitates and reflects the Triune God.

MUSICAL GARDEN OF THE HOME

From the moment the ears are formed, a child is learning by rhythms and sounds. This makes the atmosphere of the home the main source of early music exposure for any child. But it takes more than the radio to nurture this phase with good results. It also takes more than simply music.

The home should be like a garden where creativity, exploration and play are fostered. These things all reflect the nature of God and lead into a life of being mini creators like Him. Music making and listening in the home needs to be geared towards reinforcing faithful training of young children to be like their Heavenly Father. God speaks worlds into existence, and children need to be doing this on a smaller scale through play and make believe activities. One of the first signs that the garden is rich appears when parents hear their children playing in the next room while they hum or create a simple song to narrate their activities of play. They have naturally paired their storytelling with song because they cannot help being little creators when given the chance.

The home is also where most of the spoken language is learned, mom and dad and siblings as the main sources of learning. For the Christian family where one or both of the parents may not be particularly skilled in music, it is helpful to consider music in this way. This means that one can cultivate a musical culture in the home even if there is a lack of training and understanding. Saturation is the name of the game. Mom, Dad, Grandma, Grandpa and others should be singing and playing music in and around home life. Just like children are spoken to and read thousands of words, so then should parents place them in a musical world where they can begin to grow. As parents do not speak to their children only in Shakespearean prose to produce the highest aptitude for language, so music does not have to be lofty to give them similar saturation. A family uses lazy English expressions, tells stories and jokes, so also casual folk tunes and instrumental blues can teach a child a bit more about music. The focus should not be on what genre(s) to listen to, but on what music practice best reflects the Triune God. He is certainly a God of variety and fun and creativity and depth. That should be the focus of music in the home. Like immersion in a spoken language, music will seep in naturally.

In addition to this, children need to see their parents singing in church and growing in understanding of what it means to participate joyfully in the worship at church. This can not be preached with words only. It must be lived out before any words are given on the subject. The Scriptural command is for all to sing hymns, Psalms and spiritual songs, and the chief place that this happens each week is through corporate worship on the Lord's Day. Showing your children their central identity is as worshipers automatically assigns value to singing.

MUSIC EDUCATION: Training Doers of Music

As children move on to more formal instruction, it can be difficult for parents to choose which way to send them. This school has a music program, that one has band, this co-op boasts a violin instructor, private lessons have other appeal and so on. What are the key components of music training to look for when parents are deciding what to do with their young musicians?

Children need training that is meant to make them doers of music not just knowledgeable about it from a textbook, recording or performance. This means that music training in the schools should consist of sequential lessons that bring children from singing and making music to gradual awareness of what and how they are making that music, giving them building blocks in the process for future growth. They do not all have to be vocational musicians, but they should all be given the tools to be musical in whatever vocations the Lord calls them. Full music literacy means having the ability to read, write and create music. Look for music programs that direct your child in this way.

Here is a word of caution about one of the common mistakes made by eager parents. Often those who want their children to be musical enroll them in private lessons from the age of 3 or 4 thinking this is necessary to put their child on the path to musicianship. This is not an automatic path to music literacy and full musicianship. Usually their child will receive good technical training in the playing of their instrument but often this is without the cultivation of musicianship. The child will likely have an imbalance between literacy and simple, mechanical skills. Button-pushers perform with technique but do not necessarily become creators of music, able to improvise, analyze and understand their ability in light of their calling, namely to be imitators of God. Are private lessons a bad thing? Absolutely not. Just keep in mind that they are not the complete package, and seek to provide your children with music training from all sides—for their voices, their minds, their hands, their ears, their hearts. Such is the way for them to love the Lord their God with all their heart, soul, mind and strength.

APPENDIX C:
To the Church

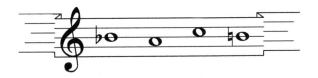

For a revival in music training to be most effective, the Church must play an important role. The Christian Church was once an active steward of the arts because art was understood to be a part of the work and purpose of the Church. Everything from music to sculpture was largely commissioned and financed by the Church, especially in the High Middle Ages and Baroque time periods of music. There are fewer and fewer churches today with well trained musicians on staff, serving in an official capacity.

Musicians like Bach worked for church, court, and city officials which provided accountability, inspiration and compensation for the professional musician. Most people today are familiar with the term "starving musician" referring to those who create and work on their own inspiration and financing. This is hardly secure as a vocation, but when the job is no longer valued, such is the result. Historically, the musician who worked under the authority of another flourished the most. When music is lacking in a culture, the Christian Church can be the most effective in giving value to such a calling again.

PATRONS AGAIN

The Church needs to communicate the importance of singing and music education in the life of the Church, and she is well poised to do it. Music training can be largely supported by the work and outsourcing of the Church in ways other civic organizations cannot support it. No other group, no matter how enthusiastic, has the same lasting motivation to support the arts as God's people.

There are many things she can do to demonstrate the high priority of music training. Churches need to be places that are friendly to concerts, private lessons and vocational music work. They can allow their instruments to be used for private lessons. They can offer a place for children's choirs and other music groups to rehearse for little or no cost. Even non-Christians will trickle in for use of a good facility. What better way to rub shoulders with the community? Churches can put on music camps and conferences where they bring in trained musicians to help local congregations grow in musicianship.

VOCATIONAL CHURCH MUSIC: Filling the Music Needs in the Church

The church can seek to have a trained musician or music minister on staff working alongside the leadership of the church. These chief musicians can help with the worship of the church and its musical discipleship. In a larger church, a chief musician might oversee other musicians, facilitating rehearsal together for worship, work with the pastoral leadership in worship music selection, and so forth. If a chief musician can also compose, he can produce tailored pieces for his particular congregation or choir for the numerous festivals and church calendar days. Overseeing the use and proper maintenance of the grander instruments could also fall under this position. Paying for such work gives value and importance to the vocations of musician, composer, music teacher, choirmaster, etc. Importance must be placed on this principle of vocational music working under the oversight of the church, for music to flourish again.

Some might object to this because of the tendancy of churches to hire professional musicians from outside the church to handle these duties. This is not a call for more churches to hire talented pianists, organists and choir directors fresh out of the local college or university. Quite the opposite, the church needs to look for people who can fill this role in a similar way they look for a pastor. Churches do not just hire any common public speaker because they are a good orator to come in and handle the preaching duties. Of course, the scrutiny and theological standards are not the same for the musician, but he should at least be someone of like mind who can work under the pastoral leadership of the church to help mature and grow the flock. Ideally, if a church is going to hire a musician to lead its church body, such a person also needs to be or become part of that congregation.

Practically, a church may not be able to quickly overhaul its staff budgets and have a full-time chief musician or music minister. Maybe the church pays to have a piece written and taught to their children's choir. Maybe it pays a musician to come in and give a concert during the Easter season on the church's piano or organ. These little steps are a great way to re-acclimate churches to the idea of vocational church music.

TRAINING ITS PARISHIONERS

In a day and age where fewer and fewer people are participating in singing in the Christian service, the Church needs to take seriously the responsibility to teach and train its parishioners in how to worship well. The Church first prepares God's people to serve the community during the week by faithful worship of the Triune God on the Lord's day. There is a need for schooling in music, primarily so that the Church can respond again in song the way she has been called to do. This means that the Lord's Day church service needs to be filled with people who have been equipped to make music.

Early Americans learned to sing the hymns and Psalms of the Church using shape notes and other symbols to teach the parts of these hymns and fuguing tunes. The music of William Billings and others from this period showed how church singing education can foster a growth in participation and composition of new tunes and hymns for edification of the church body.

Whether it is children's choir classes or adult singing practice for songs used in the service, the time would not be wasted if your people are gathering and practicing to come into the sanctuary with preparation and joy. Or why not take advantage of the Sunday school hour to help disciple the congregation? The church's practice of discipleship through Sunday classes on specific topics and Bible study is a healthy one and one that can be helpful in the musical discipleship of the church. Use whatever opportunities fit your congregation.

About the Author

JARROD RICHEY has been teaching K4 through 12th grade general music and choir at Geneva Academy in Monroe, LA since 2008. He is the founder and director of the Delta Youth Chorale, a children's community choir that promotes music literacy through singing, folk dance and activities. Additionally, Mr. Richey has directed choir and taught voice and music appreciation classes at the University of Louisiana at Monroe. He received his bachelor's degree at Louisiana Tech University before completing his Masters of Music at the University of Louisiana at Monroe. He also completed his national Kodály music teacher certification from Wichita State University. He is an active choir clinician and speaker. He also serves on the executive board of the Louisiana chapters of the Organization of American Kodály Educators and the American Choral Directors Association. Jarrod and his lovely wife, Sarah, have five young choristers in training.